SNOWBOARDING

GILLIAN C. P. BROWN

HIGH
interest
books

Children's Press®
A Division of Scholastic Inc.

New York ... Toronto ... London ... Auckland ... Sydney
Mexico City ... New Delhi ... Hong Kong

Book Design: Michael DeLisio
Contributing Editor: Scott Waldman
Photo Credits: Cover © Russi/ImageState; back cover © Duomo/Corbis; title
page, p. 3 © Eyewire; p. 5 © Sport the Library/Icon SMI; p. 6 © Horace Bristol/
Corbis; pp. 11, 16, 19, 26, 28, 32, 37 © AP/Wide World Photos; pp. 12, 22
© Icon SMI; p. 15 © Ales Fevzer/Corbis; p. 17 Michael DeLisio; p. 21 © Brian
Bahr/Getty Images; p. 25 © Mike Cooper/Getty Images; p. 31 © Affleck/
ImageState; p. 34 © William Sallaz/Corbis; p. 38 © ImageState

Library of Congress Cataloging-in-Publication Data

Brown, Gillian (Gillian C. P.)
    Snowboarding / Gillian Brown.
    p. cm. — (X-treme outdoors)
    Includes bibliographical references and index.
    Contents: X-treme challenge — A day at the races — Getting geared up
    — Suit up and ride!
    ISBN 0-516-24322-5 (lib. bdg.) — ISBN 0-516-24383-7 (pbk.)
    1. Snowboarding—Juvenile literature. [1. Snowboarding.] I. Title:
    Snowboarding. II. Title. III. Series.

GV857.S57 .B77 2003
796.9—dc21
                                                    2002010891

CONTENTS

INTRODUCTION

The sound of the winter wind fills your ears. Snow falls gently on the mountain slope all around you, building up in soft, powdery layers. Here, at the top of the mountain, you're at the same height as the clouds. Taking a deep breath of cool, fresh air, you slide your goggles down over your eyes. Looming below you is a few thousand feet of untouched snow. Your friend gives you a nod and pushes off into the white powder. You follow, your board gliding easily over the top of the snow. As you pick up speed, the world becomes a blur. You carve back and forth to control your speed. Suddenly, a large mogul appears directly in your path. No problem—you soar over it and turn around 360 degrees while you're in the air. Your landing in a pile of unpacked snow feels like jumping on a featherbed. A rush of adrenaline washes over your body as you pick up speed again and look for the next mogul. Welcome to the exciting world of snowboarding!

Catch air one time on a snowboard and you'll be hooked forever.

The sport of snowboarding might be new, but it has caught on quickly. Millions of people worldwide enjoy snowboarding each year. Snowboarding involves a lot of risk, so snowboarders need special skills. This book will answer many of the questions you might have about snowboarding: How did this sport grow so fast? What kind of equipment do I need? How are competitions run? Where can I snowboard? Who's the best snowboarder today?

Let's leap into the *X-treme* world of snowboarding —a fast world filled with thrills and challenges, competitions and cool gear, superstars and fantastic tricks.

CHAPTER ONE

X-TREME CHALLENGE

People have been making tools to glide over snow for thousands of years. Ancient skis have been found in Scandinavian and Finnish bogs. Petroglyphs have also been found in Norway. This evidence indicates that humans developed skis over 5,000 years ago. Skiing developed into a popular hobby in the twentieth century. It was only natural that people would soon think up new and more exciting ways to cruise down snow-covered slopes.

One of the earliest snowboards dates back to 1929. A man named M.J. Burchett attached a piece of plywood to his feet using clothesline and horse reins. Burchett was able to glide over the snow on his new

The popularity of skiing in the last hundred years led to the development of snowboarding.

invention. Snowboarding as you know it today started in Michigan in 1965. Sherman Poppen made a snowboard out of two skis that he screwed together. He called his new invention a "snurfer," which is a combination of the words *snow* and *surfer*. Over the next ten years, almost one million snurfers were sold in North America. Many people started to surf on snow. Some of them began to make better snowboards. Many of these new snowboard fanatics started their own snowboard-manufacturing companies in the early 1980s.

In 1987, magazines such as *TransWorld Snowboarding* and *Snowboarder Magazine* started promoting this new sport to skateboarders, surfers, and skiers. In 1994, the *Wall Street Journal* said, "Snowboarding scores as the fastest growing sport with participation up fifty percent since the previous winter."

Sports such as snowboarding are exciting because they are new and very challenging. They offer an adventurous alternative to traditional organized sports, such as basketball and soccer. Snowboarding is fun because an individual is constantly pushed to learn new things—such as trying new tricks, riding a halfpipe, or conquering a black diamond run.

As you will learn in this book, halfpipes are large U-shaped valleys of snow. Black diamonds are the most difficult hills in snowboarding areas.

At the 1998 Winter Olympics in Nagano, Japan, snowboarding was added as an official sport. Today, you can watch snowboarding on ESPN and MTV. Snowboarding is also featured in a lot of advertising. Teenagers and adults who want to try something new and extreme help make snowboarding one of the most popular new sports in the world.

X-FACTOR

Each trail at all snowboarding areas is rated for its level of difficulty. The trails are marked with different symbols. A green circle indicates an easy trail, meant for beginners. A blue square means the trail is of intermediate difficulty. A black diamond indicates the most difficult trail, meant only for experienced snowboarders. The ratings are unique to each ski area, so a blue square in Utah might be as difficult as a black diamond in Minnesota.

The most challenging snowboarding in the world can be found in Alaska, New Zealand, Chile, and the Alps in Europe. Many of these areas can only be reached by helicopter! In heli-skiing, a helicopter drops snowboarders or skiers at the top of a mountain. This is one of the most exciting kinds of snowboarding because there are no marked trails at that extreme height. Snowboarding, however, is enjoyable on any level, from beginner to pro. Almost anyone can snowboard. Of course, you'll need to be in an area where there is snow or where snow can be made. There are snowboard areas in the mountains and even in places with flatter land, such as Iowa.

Safety is top priority in sports such as snowboarding. It is important for snowboarders to know local weather conditions before they hit the slopes. They need to know how cold temperatures will be so they can wear the right clothing. They also need to know if any storms have been predicted so that they can make decisions about where and when to snowboard. For people snowboarding in the mountains, avalanche safety is very important. This means knowing all about the snow conditions and where

These rescue workers are helping people trapped by an avalanche. Snowboarders have to be aware of avalanche areas to avoid accidents like this one.

avalanches are most likely to happen. Snowboarders often carry safety equipment, such as shovels and transceivers. A transceiver is a small electronic device that can help locate a person trapped by an avalanche.

CHAPTER TWO

A DAY AT THE RACES

There are many different types of snowboarding competitions. Some competitions are based on speed. Two examples of speed competitions are the giant slalom in the Winter Olympics and the Snowboarder X at the Winter X Games. In these two competitions, snowboarders race one at a time downhill. The snowboarder who makes it to the bottom in the fastest time is the winner.

There are also competitions based on style. In these competitions, judges decide which snowboarder does the best tricks. The halfpipe and slopestyle competitions at the U.S. Open Snowboarding Championships are examples of style competitions.

Snowboarders practice the same tricks for many years before perfecting them.

The X Games and the Winter Olympics also feature style competitions. Some competitions are based on how high the snowboarders can leap! These competitions are often called big air. The Gravity Games Big Air competition is an example of this.

SPEED COMPETITIONS

Snowboarding speed competitions are similar to downhill ski races. A speed course has poles, called gates, that the snowboarder has to weave between. Good downhill courses have many hills and a variety of short, medium, and long turns. In the giant slalom, a snowboarder races against the clock down a course that is between 656 to 1,312 feet (200 to 399.9 meters) long. The snowboarder must also race on two different courses. The winner of the competition is the person who completes both courses the fastest.

The Snowboarder X is a speed competition, but with one big difference: Six snowboarders all race at the same time! The snowboarders zoom down a race course with jumps that the snowboarders must ride over.

Some snowboard races, such as this one, have obstacles in the middle of the course.

Contestants in a halfpipe competition often jump two or three times their height to perform tricks.

STYLE COMPETITIONS

The halfpipe is probably the best-known snowboard competition. In the 2002 Winter Olympics, the halfpipe was up to 59 feet (18 m) wide, 15 feet (4.6 m) high, and 394 feet (120.1 m) long. Each snowboarder gets three runs and is scored by a panel of judges.

Another competition based on style is the slopestyle contest in which competitors take three runs down a course filled with jumps, rails, and quarterpipes. The course has a minimum of six elements and must be at least 98 feet wide (29.9 m) and 492 feet (150 m) long. Judges score the snowboarder on overall impression. The overall impression includes sequence, amount of risk, type of tricks, and use of the slopestyle elements on the course.

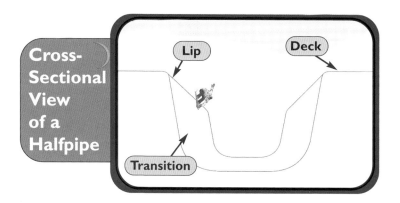

CATCHING AIR

Big air contests challenge snowboarders to launch themselves sky high, pull an awesome trick 50 feet (15.2 m) in the air, land smoothly, and ride away. The Gravity Games, the World Snowboarding Championship, and the Vans Triple Crown feature this type of competition. Big air snowboarders are truly *X-treme* athletes. Their daring moves wow crowds everywhere. Winners of these awe-inspiring events walk away with thousands of dollars in prize money.

KNOW THE LINGO

Halfpipe action has a language of its own. Here are some terms used to describe life in the halfpipe:

- *Dropping* is when a snowboarder goes down into the halfpipe.

- A *hit* is when a snowboarder does a trick in the air.

- A *straight air* happens when a snowboarder rises into the air, turns 180 degrees, and drops back into the halfpipe. This is the most basic maneuver in the halfpipe.

- A *grab* is when a snowboarder reaches down and grabs onto his or her snowboard. There are many different kinds of grabs with names such as stalefish, mute, tail, nose, and method.

- A *spin* is when a snowboarder rotates his or her snowboard. Spins are named by the number of degrees the snowboarder covers during the spin. For example, one full spin is a 360 or a "3." Two full spins are a 540 or a "5."

- *Frontside* and *backside* refer to the snowboard edges on the snow. The frontside edge is where the toes are and the backside is where the heels are.

- *Sketch* or *sketchy* is used to describe the snowboarder being off balance, though not necessarily falling down.

Stine Kjeldass is pulling a grab as she struggles to outdo her competitors.

THE BIG DEAL: THE U.S. OPEN SNOWBOARDING CHAMPIONSHIPS

Since 1982, the best snowboarders in the world have gathered in mid-March at Stratton Mountain in Vermont to compete in the U.S. Open Snowboarding Championships. For snowboarders, this event is the most important competition of the year. More than five hundred male and female snowboarders from more than fifteen countries take part in the halfpipe and slopestyle competitions.

The U.S. Open is an exciting and challenging week of competition. Snowboarders arrive on Monday or Tuesday to practice in the halfpipe at Stratton Mountain. On Wednesday, they practice again and participate in the prequalifier competitions. Prequalifiers are held to see who will make it to the quarterfinals held later in the week. On Thursday and Friday, there is more halfpipe practice. The quarterfinals and semifinals are both held on Friday.

Finally, on Saturday afternoon, the halfpipe finals are held. Music by rock bands, such as Korn and Blink 182, blares out of loudspeakers. A crowd of 20,000 spectators cheer as the finalists ride the halfpipe for all they're worth.

Ross Powers' performance at events such as the U. S. Open helped earn him a spot on the 2002 U. S. Winter Olympic team.

The 2002 men's halfpipe champion at the U.S. Open was Danny Kass, from New Jersey. Danny's nickname is "Big Dan." He is known for his complicated tricks and solid landings. Though only twenty years old, he beat the competition at the 2002 U.S. Open by pulling off two superhuman tricks. In one of these tricks, Danny spun around three times upside down! Danny also won a silver medal for his halfpipe performance at the 2002 Winter Olympics in Salt Lake City, Utah. At age nineteen, Danny was the youngest member of the 2002 U.S. Olympic men's snowboarding team. He was the halfpipe champion at both the 2001 X Games and the 2001 U.S. Open. Also, Danny invented the Kasserole. It's one of his signature moves that is often described as a human kick-flip.

The 2002 U.S. Open women's halfpipe champion was Kelly Clark from Mt. Snow, Vermont. Clark is known for the incredible amplitude she achieves. Amplitude is the height above the lip of the halfpipe that a snowboarder jumps. At the U.S. Open, Clark pulled off a series of nearly impossible tricks, even scraping her face in one fall. At only eighteen years old, Clark also won the gold medal in the halfpipe at

Tricks such as this earned Danny Kass a silver medal in the 2002 Winter Olympics.

the 2002 Winter Olympics. At the Olympics, everyone agreed that Clark's performance pushed women's snowboarding to new heights.

Terje Haakonsen is thought by many people to be the most famous snowboarder ever. He is truly a legend. Haakonsen won the U.S. Open halfpipe competition three times, the World Snowboarding Championships five times, and the Mt. Baker Banked Slalom four times. Haakonsen was born in Telemark, Norway. He is known for his natural athleticism and confidence that he blends with a playful approach to snowboarding. Whether he's on the slopes or in the halfpipe, Haakonsen rides with the same enthusiasm. Today, he plans different snow-boarding events, such as the Arctic Challenge held in the Lofoten Islands of Norway. He still rides in many different competitions.

Terje Haakonsen catches air off the halfpipe during the 1995 World Snowboard Championships.

CHAPTER THREE

GEARING UP

Before you buy any snowboarding gear, take a lesson or two. You can rent a board and boots, then spend a few days hitting the slopes to see if snowboarding is for you. If you enjoy the thrill of being on a board, you will probably want to go snowboarding again in the future. That might be the time to buy some gear of your own.

The snowboard you will use depends on what type of snowboarding you will be doing. To ride a halfpipe you need a board that is flexible and designed for performing tricks. This kind of board is called a freestyle board. Freestyle snowboards are what most beginners use. If speed is what you're after, you're better off with a carving board. Carving boards are designed for speed and tend to be more rigid than freestyle boards. On a carving board, turning at high speeds is easier.

Rent a board and get out on the slopes for a few days before you decide to invest in snowboarding gear.

A freeride board is a blend of the freestyle board and the carving board. Both ends of this board are turned up, making going backward or forward easier. Freeride boards are the most stable at high speeds. They are easier to ride through a greater variety of snow conditions than other boards.

Bindings keep your feet attached to the snowboard. Good bindings are strong as well as flexible. There are four types of bindings. One type of binding is called freestyle binding. It has three straps that hold the boot onto the board. Another type of binding is called a step-in binding. The boot clicks into the binding on top of the board. Two other types of binding are the hard-boot and soft-boot bindings. The hard-boot binding is used for high-speed carving and racing. It has two small clips that hold the boot to the board. The soft-boot binding is very similar to the freestyle binding, except that it has only two straps.

There are two different kinds of boots: one designed for the freestyle binding, and one designed to click into the step-in binding. The boots that fit into the freestyle bindings are the more flexible of the two. Whichever boot and binding system feels the best for

These are just a few of the many different types of snowboard.

you is the right system. Snowboarders who do lots of tricks may choose the freestyle binding and boots. This is because they can bend their ankles more. They can also feel the small movements of their board better. A snowboarder who wants the ease of getting in and out of his or her bindings quickly might choose the step-in bindings and boots.

The gear you need to keep yourself safe and warm is called soft goods. Helmets, goggles, wrist guards, and knee pads are soft goods designed to keep you safe from injury. Coats, snow pants, hats, gloves, socks, and long underwear are soft goods needed to keep you warm.

Snowboarders get ready for the slopes by dressing in three layers. For the first layer, a snowboarder wears long underwear and warm socks made of wool or synthetic material. Clothing made of synthetic material will keep you warm even when it's wet. It also dries quickly. It's a better choice than cotton because cotton takes a long time to dry and will not keep you warm when it's wet. The next layer is a coat, snow pants, and gloves. This outer layer is waterproof and windproof. It keeps a snowboarder dry and warm in icy winter weather. The final layer is the helmet, goggles, wrist

Staying warm on the slopes is an important part of staying
safe when you're out snowboarding.

guards, and knee pads. This equipment should fit comfortably and snugly. You don't want these pieces to fly off if you take a spill.

Bindings, boots, and snowboards are generally sold separately. Getting started in snowboarding can cost anywhere from a few hundred dollars to over a thousand dollars. A decent beginner's board usually costs over $200. To make snowboarding more affordable, many beginners buy used gear. Be a smart buyer when shopping for a used board. Check for deep scrapes and cracks on the board. Make sure the edges are thick because they can wear out. Place the board on the ground and make sure that it arches slightly under the center. Boards that sit flat are worn out and will not turn properly. Try rocking the board gently. Both edges at the tip and tail should touch the ground. If the board rocks from side to side, it probably is bent.

Test your equipment before you hit the slopes. Your bindings should be in working order and your straps should fit snugly on your feet.

CHAPTER FOUR

SUIT UP AND RIDE!

Now that you know the basics of snowboarding, what do you need to do to get out on the slopes? That's easy: Find a snowboard area that is close to you. Check out its Web site or call to see what kind of beginner's deals it offers. Most ski and snowboard areas have a first timer's rental, lesson, and lift ticket package available. Generally, these packages can cost between $40 to $125. Snowboard areas want you to learn how to snowboard so that you will come back again and again. If you do your research, you will find that there are many small snowboard areas that are the perfect places to learn.

Taking a lesson is the easiest and safest way to learn how to snowboard. Learning from a pro will

The only way to become as good as the pros is to get out on the slopes and ride!

make it easier for you to have fun on a snowboard. You'll get hands-on instruction from an experienced snowboarder—and a partner who wants to share the fun of snowboarding with you.

The most important snowboarding skills to learn are starting, stopping, and steering a snowboard. You'll also learn the skills to handle ice, steep trails, and high speeds. An American Association of Snowboard Instructors (AASI) certified instructor has the special training to teach you everything you'll need on the slopes.

Learning to snowboard takes time and patience. After your first lesson, you should go snowboarding again as soon as you can. This will help you to practice what you've learned. You will be amazed at how easily you can learn to snowboard after just a couple of days on the snow.

Snowboarding is a great way to meet people who share your interests. There may be a group in your town that goes snowboarding regularly. Check out the Yellow Pages, the Internet, local newspapers, and recreation centers to find one. You can also talk to the staff at your local board shop. They can tell you a lot

It's important to be patient while you're learning how to ride a snowboard. It may take a little while, but you'll get the hang of it.

about snowboarding areas close to home. They'll also know about the newest boots, bindings, and boards. Magazines such as *TransWorld* and *Snowboarder* are filled with awesome pictures and lots of information about the world of snowboarding. You can also surf the Web and learn a lot about this great sport.

Snowboarding is *X-treme* because it is filled with risks, cool tricks, and beautiful outdoor scenery. It is easy to learn and is a great way to get outside and play. Learn more about snowboarding and then take a lesson. Soon you'll be on your way to the best winter thrill around!

Once your friends hear about how much fun you had on a snowboard, they'll want to come along next time!

NEW WORDS

amplitude the height a snowboarder jumps above the lip of the halfpipe

avalanche a large mass of snow that breaks loose and moves swiftly down the side of a mountain

carve to weave back and forth on your snowboard while going downhill

elements different pieces or parts of a whole

gear equipment or clothing needed for a sport, such as a snowboard for snowboarding

intermediate in between two things or in the middle

lingo language used and understood only by people in a certain work, activity, or sport

NEW WORDS

maneuver a difficult movement that needs planning and skill

mogul a large bump on a ski hill made out snow and ice

petroglyphs carvings on a rock

protective in snowboarding, this describes equipment that protects the snowboarder from the snow and cold as well as injury

slalom a timed race over a winding course

synthetic describing something that is man-made

terrain the features of a piece of land

FOR FURTHER READING

Hart, Lowell. *The Snowboard Book: A Guide for All Boarders.* New York: W.W. Norton, 1997.

Jensen, Julie, and Jon Lurie. *Beginning Snowboarding.* Minneapolis, MN: The Lerner Publishing Group, 1995.

Malthouse, Becci, and Sang Tan. *Extreme Sports: Snowboarding.* Hauppauge, NY: Barron's Educational Series, 1998.

Masoff, Joy. *Snowboard! Extreme Sports: Your Guide to Freeriding, Pipe & Park, Jibbing, Backcountry, Alpine, Boardercross, and More.* Washington, DC: National Geographic Society, 2002.

FOR FURTHER READING

Maurer, Tracy Nelson. *Snowboarding.* Vero Beach, FL: Rourke Publishing, 2002.

Miller, Chuck. *Snowboarding.* Austin, TX: Raintree Steck-Vaughn Publishers, 2002.

Ryan, Patrick. *Extreme Snowboarding.* Mankato, MN: Capstone Press, 1998.

RESOURCES

Organizations

Professional Snowboarders Association of North America

P.O. Box 477
Vail, CO 81658
(303) 949-5473

United States Ski and Snowboard Association

P.O. Box 100
1500 Kearns Boulevard
Park City, UT 84060
(801) 649-9090

RESOURCES

Web Sites
U.S. Open
www.usopen-snowboarding.com
This Web site has information and updates on the athletes and the competitions that are part of the U.S. Open.

X Games
http://expn.go.com/snb/
The X Games is one of the most exciting sporting events shown on ESPN. Learn all about the X Games snowboarding competitions on this site.

Snowboarding
www.snowboarding.com
This site provides snowboarding news from all around the world and information about the biggest events.

RESOURCES

Snowlink

www.snowlink.com

This Web site has information on many different types of snow sports. Learn about clubs and activities in your area.

Ski Odyssey

http://www.skiodyssey.com/usamap.cfm

This site has maps and phone numbers of all the ski areas in the United States.

Transworld Snowboarding

www.transworldsnowboarding.com

This link will take you to the magazine with all you'll ever need to know about snowboarding.

INDEX

INDEX

About the Author

Gillian C.P. Brown is a Level 1 AASI Certitified Snowboard Instructor. She has lived and worked in Colorado, California, Wisconsin, and New York. She is now a freelance writer who is studying poetry in the Master of Arts program at the City University of New York - City College.